Copyright

I0473433

All rights reserved. No part of this book may be reproduced or transmitted in any

form without permission from the publisher, except as permitted by U.K.

copyright law.

For permissions contact: kieran@preeminenceconsulting.com

2

Table of Contents

4

Glossary

- **Data controller** – A person or body, alone or jointly, which determines the purposes and means of processing personal data.
- **Data processor** – An entity which processes the data on behalf of the data controller.
- **Personal data** – Any information relating to an identified/identifiable, natural person, a "data subject". A data subject is a natural person, who can be identified, or is identifiable, directly or indirectly.
- **Special categories of data** – Known as "sensitive data". The GDPR has extended the definition to include both biometric and genetic data.

6

Principles relating to the processing of personal data

Personal data shall be:

- Processed lawfully, fairly and in a transparent manner

- Collected for specified, explicit and legitimate purposes and not further processed in a manner that is incompatible with those purposes

- Adequate, relevant and limited to what is necessary in relation to the purposes for which they are processed

- Accurate and where necessary, kept up to date

- Kept in a form permitting identification of data subjects not longer than necessary for the purposes for which the personal data are processed

- Processed in a manner that ensures appropriate security of the personal data, using appropriate technical and organisational measures.

The data controller shall be responsible for, and able to demonstrate compliance with the above.

8

Lawfulness of processing

Processing is lawful if:

- Consent is given by the data subject
- For the performance of a contract to which the data subject is a party or in order to take steps at the request of the data subject prior to entering into a contract
- In compliance with a legal obligation to which the controller is subject.
- To protect the vital interests of the data subject or other natural person
- For the performance of a task carried out in the public interest or in the exercise of official authority vested in the controller
- For the purposes of legitimate interests pursued by the controller or a third party, except where such interests are overridden by the interests or fundamental rights and freedoms of the data subject.

10

Consent

Consent must be:

- Freely given

- Specific

- Informed

- Unambiguous – clear affirmative action

- Capable of withdrawal at any time

- Demonstrable

- Presented in a manner which is clearly distinguishable from other matters in an intelligible and easily accessible form, using clear and plain language.

12

Information duty (Right to be informed)

Obligation for the controller to inform the data subject on:

- The identity and contact details of the controller and where applicable the Data Protection Officer

- The purpose for processing and the legal basis for processing personal data

- Where the processing is based on your legitimate interests or the legitimate interests of a third party, the legitimate interest pursued by you or by the third party

- Any recipient or categories of recipients of the personal data

- If transferring data to third countries: the appropriate or suitable safeguards for the protection of this data

- The period for which the personal data will be stored; or if that is not possible, the criteria used to determine the period

- The existence of the data subject's right to request access to, rectify, and erase personal data, to restrict the processing, to object to processing of personal data on grounds related to the data subject's situation, and the right to data portability

- Where the processing is based on consent, the right to withdraw to consent at any time

- The right to complain to a supervisory authority and contact details of the authority

- Whether the provision of personal data is part of a statutory or contractual requirement or obligation and possible consequences of failing to provide the personal data

- If relevant: details regarding automated decision-making, including profiling, and, in such case, information on the logic involved as well as the significance and envisaged consequences of such profiling for the data subject

- When data has not been obtained directly from the data subject: from which source the personal data originates, and if applicable, whether it came from publicly accessible sources.

The data subject shall be informed if the personal data is to be processed for a purpose other than which the personal data was originally collected.

The information shall be given in a concise, transparent, intelligible and easily accessible form using clear and plain language.

The information shall be given when the personal data is obtained (if the personal data is obtained from the data subject) or within one month (if not collected from the data subject) or at the latest at the first communication or disclosure of the personal data. This shall not apply if the data subject already has the information or the provision of such information proves impossible or would involve a disproportionate effort.

Right of access

Right of data subject to get information on:

- Whether or not personal data on the data subject is being processed
- Information on the processing – purpose, categories, recipients etc…
- A copy of the personal data undergoing processing: (a) must be provided to the data subject (b) providing the personal data must not adversely affect the rights and freedoms of others.

Requested by electronic means: the personal data must be provided in a commonly used electronic form. Must be provided within one month and may be extended by an additional two months. The first copy of the personal data must be provided free of charge.

Exception from the right of access: the request is manifestly unfounded or excessive (i.e. repetitive).

16

Right to rectification

The data subject shall have the right:

- To have personal data rectified without delay
- To have incomplete personal data completed.

Any rectification of the personal data shall be communicated to the recipients the personal data has already been disclosed to, unless this proves impossible or involves a disproportionate effort.

18

Right to erasure

Personal data shall be erased without delay if:

- The personal data is no longer necessary to achieve the purpose for which it was collected or otherwise processed
- The data subject withdraws their consent on which the processing was based and where there is no other legal grounds for the processing
- The data subject objects to the processing and there are no overriding legitimate grounds for the processing
- The personal data has been unlawfully processed
- The personal data has to be erased for compliance with a legal obligation.

The obligation also applies if the personal data has been made public or transferred to other controllers.

Exceptions: the personal data is necessary for the establishment, exercise or defence of legal claims, or for the compliance with a legal obligation which requires processing etc…

The controller has a duty to take reasonable steps to inform those processing the personal data that the data subject has requested the erasure.

20

Right to restriction of processing

May be required by data subject if:

- The accuracy of the personal data is contested by the data subject (until the accuracy of the personal data is verified)
- The processing is unlawful and the data subject opposes the erasure of the personal data and requests the restriction of its use instead
- The controller no longer needs the personal data for the purposes of the processing, but it is required by the data subject for the establishment, exercise or defence of legal claims
- The data subject has objected to the processing pursuant to Article 21 (Right to object) pending verification as to whether the legitimate grounds of the controller override those of the data subject.

Where processing has been restricted, such personal data shall, with the exception of storage, only be processed with the data subjects consent or for the establishment, exercise or defence of legal claims or for the protection of the rights of another natural or legal person.

A data subject who has obtained restriction of processing shall be informed by the controller before the restriction of processing is lifted.

Any restriction of personal data shall be communicated to recipients to which the personal data has already been disclosed to, unless this proves impossible or involves disproportionate effort.

Right to data portability

Must be provided in a structured, commonly used machine-readable format.

Applies only to personal data that the data subject has provided to a controller, and provided that:

- The processing is based on consent or on a contract

- The processing is carried out by automated means.

24

Right to object

Data subject may object at any time if the processing is based on public interest/official authority or legitimate interest.

Processing for direct marketing purposes may always be objected to.

There is an exception if it is demonstrated that there are compelling legitimate grounds for the processing which override the interests, rights and freedoms of the data subject, or for the establishment, exercise or defence of legal claims.

26

Rights related to automated individual decision making including profiling

The data subject shall not be subject to decisions based solely on automated processing, including profiling, which produces legal effects or has similarly significantly affects.

Automated individual decision making including profiling shall not be based on special categories of personal data unless suitable measures to safeguard the data subject's rights and freedoms and legitimate interests are in place.

Exceptions: (i) necessary for contract or performance of a contract, (ii) authorised by law to which the controller is subject and which also lays down suitable measures to safeguard the data subject's rights and legitimate interests, or (iii) based on the data subject's explicit consent.

For exceptions controller shall implement suitable measures to safeguard the data subject's rights and legitimate interests, including at least the right to obtain human intervention on the part of the controller, to express the data subject's point of view and to contest the decision.

28

Security of personal data

Data controller must implement appropriate technical and organisational measures to ensure a level of security appropriate to the risk considering: nature, scope, context, purposes of the processing, risk (of varying likelihood and severity) to the rights and freedoms of data subjects (natural persons).

Organisation must be able to demonstrate performance in accordance with the GDPR, implement appropriate data protection policies, and adhere to appropriate codes of conduct and certification mechanisms (when applicable).

30

Data protection by design and default

Appropriate technical and organisational measures shall be implemented to ensure compliance with the GDPR and protect the rights of the data subject, taking into account:

- The state of the art
- The cost of implementation
- The nature, scope, context and purposes of the processing
- The risks (of varying likelihood and severity) to rights and freedoms of natural persons posed by the processing.

Ensuring that, by default, only personal data which is necessary for each specific purpose of the processing is processed, and applies to:

(i) The amount of personal data collected

(ii) The extent of its processing and the period of storage

(iii) Accessibility, in particular, such measures shall ensure that, by default, personal data is not made accessible without the individual's intervention to an indefinite number of natural persons.

32

Personal data breach

A breach of security leading to:

1. Accidental or unlawful destruction, loss, alteration, unauthorised disclosure of, or

2. Access to, personal data, transmitted, stored or otherwise processed.

The processor shall notify the personal data breach to:

- The controller without undue delay

- The supervisory authority (Data Protection Authority) not later than 72 hours after having become aware of the personal data breach unless it is unlikely to result in a risk to the rights and freedoms of natural persons

- Communicate breach to data subjects without undue delay if the breach is likely to result in a high risk to the rights and freedoms of the data subject. Not necessary if measures are taken to ensure that the high risk is not likely to materialise or would involve a disproportionate effort.

34

Data protection impact assessment (DPIA/PIA)

Used to carry out an assessment of the impact of the envisaged processing operations on the protection of personal data prior to the processing.

Processing likely to result in a high risk to the rights of natural persons.

By using new technologies, and taking into account the nature, scope, context and purposes of the processing.

Should involve the processor and the data protection officer (DPO).

Shall contain at least:

- A systematic description of envisaged processing operations and the purposes of the processing including the legitimate interest pursued
- An assessment of the necessity and proportionality of the processing operations in relation to the purposes
- An assessment of the risks to the rights and freedoms of the data subjects
- Measures envisaged to address the risks including safeguards, security measures and mechanisms to ensure protection of the personal data and to demonstrate compliance.

36

Data protection officer (DPO)

Required if:

- Processing by a public authority or body (except courts)

- Core activities require regular and systematic monitoring on a large scale

- Core activities of processing on a large of special categories of data/criminal convictions and offences.

38

Steps your organisation can take to prepare

1. **Assemble a GDPR compliance team**: Each member should act as a liaison with their respective department.

2. **Conduct an audit:** establish what data you currently hold, where it is stored, and who has access to it. Erase any unnecessary data.

3. **Know your data flows**: Evaluate what data your organisation collects from customers and employees and how data is transmitted within the EU and globally.

4. **Analyse the lawful basis on which you use personal data**.

5. **Review privacy notices:** Ensure you are providing required disclosures.

6. **Prepare for data security breaches**: Put in place policies and well-practiced procedures to ensure that you can react quickly to any data breach and notify the Data Protection Authority (ICO) in time (*within 72 Hours*), when required.

7. **Establish a framework for accountability**: Ensure that you have clear policies in place to prove that you meet required standards. Establish a culture of monitoring, reviewing and assessing your data processing procedures, aiming to minimise data processing and retention of data, and building in safeguards.

8. **Embrace privacy by design**: Ensure that privacy is embedded into any new processing or product that is developed. Implement appropriate technical and organisational measures to ensure and demonstrate that you comply i.e. data protection policies, staff training, internal audit, and reviews of HR policies.

9. **Evaluate security protocols**: Consider pseudonymising and encrypting data as well as carrying out regular testing of security programs.

10. **Consider appointing a data protection advisor/consultant.**

11. **Review agreements with processors and third-party vendors**: Ensure both are contractually required to comply with the GDPR.

12. **Have policies and procedures in place to address the rights of data subjects.**

For access to the Microsoft Powerpoint slides that are to be used in conjunction with this training booklet please email kieran@preminenceconsulting.com and include a copy of your proof of purchase.

For more detailed training and reference please see:

https://www.amazon.co.uk/GDPR-Training-Manual-Kieran-McLaughlin/dp/1096662108/

If you require additional GDPR help or would like a GDPR Compliance Audit please contact kieran@preeminenceconsulting.com

42

www.ingramcontent.com/pod-product-compliance
Lightning Source LLC
Chambersburg PA
CBHW072303170526
45158CB00003BA/1170